THE ST ELLA FITZGERALD

A Biography Book for New Readers

— Written by —
Kathy Trusty

— Illustrated by —
Sawyer Cloud

ROCKRIDGE PRESS

Series Designer: Angela Navarra
Interior and Cover Designer: Karmen Lizzul
Art Producer: Hannah Dickerson
Editor: Eliza Kirby
Production Manager: Holly Haydash
Production Editor: Melissa Edeburn

Illustrations © 2021 Sawyer Cloud; all maps used under license from Creative Market. Photography © Everett Collection Historical/Alamy Stock Photo, p. 50; Pictorial Press Ltd/Alamy Stock Photo, p. 52; Records/Alamy Stock Photo, p. 53.

Print ISBN: 978-1-64876-297-0 | eBook ISBN: 978-1-63807-280-5
R1

CONTENTS

CHAPTER 1

A "QUEEN" IS BORN

Meet Ella Fitzgerald

When Ella Fitzgerald was growing up, she loved to sing and dance. Dancing was her favorite activity. She wanted to be a famous dancer one day.

When Ella was seventeen, some friends dared her to enter a talent show. She did not want to lose the dare. She signed up, and she was picked to be in the show.

When it was Ella's turn, she walked on the stage and froze. There were so many people there. The lights were very bright. She could not make her legs move. Ella was so afraid. She just stood there. People started booing. Ella did not know what to do.

Ella was too afraid to dance, so she started singing. The audience members were surprised by her voice. They became quiet so they could hear her. Ella had a beautiful voice. When she

finished the song, the crowd clapped for so long
Ella had to sing another song. Ella could not
believe it. She won the $25 first prize.

Ella never became a famous dancer. She
became a famous singer. She sang **jazz** and
became one of the greatest jazz singers in the
United States.

She sang different types of jazz. Ella sang
swing jazz that people could dance to. She sang
bebop jazz that had a fast beat. She also sang jazz
ballads that had a slower beat. Ella made people

enjoy them all. An important feature of jazz, for Ella and other Black musicians, was the freedom to make up sounds and words as they went along.

Some people called her the "Queen of Jazz." Other people called her the "First Lady of Song." Ella and her beautiful voice entertained people for more than seventy years.

> The only thing better than singing is more singing.

Ella's America

Ella Jane Fitzgerald was born on April 25, 1917, in Newport News, Virginia. Newport News is a town near the James River in southeast Virginia.

Ella's mother's name was Temperance. Everyone called her Tempie. Her father's name was William Fitzgerald. He left the family when Ella was still a baby.

Three weeks before Ella was born, the United States **declared war** on Germany. The country had entered World War I. World War I was a battle between the biggest and most powerful countries in the world. Many of the American soldiers who fought in World War I trained in Newport News before they went to Europe to help France and England in the war.

When Ella was born, there was **racial segregation** in Virginia and in the United States army. When soldiers came to Newport News

to train for the war, Black soldiers and white soldiers trained in separate areas.

There was segregation in other places, too. Black and white children could not go to the same schools in Virginia. Black people and white people had to sit in different sections on **streetcars**. There were signs showing Black

How would you feel if you could not sit any place you wanted on a bus?

passengers where to sit. If a Black person sat in the white section, they would have been breaking the law.

The laws that separated Black people and white people were called **"Jim Crow" laws**. People still had to follow those rules in many places around the country when Ella was growing up.

WHEN?

The United States declares war on Germany.	Ella Fitzgerald is born	American soldiers arrive in Europe.
APRIL 6, 1917	**APRIL 25, 1917**	**JUNE 24, 1917**

BENJAMIN FRANKLIN JUNIOR HIGH GLEE CLUB

CHAPTER 2

THE EARLY YEARS

Growing Up in Yonkers

When Ella was three years old, she and her mom, Tempie, moved to New York.

They were part of the Great Migration. The Great Migration happened between 1915 and 1970. Millions of Black people left the South and moved to cities in the North. They were looking for better opportunities for their families.

The Fitzgerald Family Tree

JOSEPH DA SILVA (UNKNOWN)	VIRGINIA (UNKNOWN)	TEMPERANCE FITZGERALD (?-1932)	WILLIAM FITZGERALD (UNKNOWN)

FRANCES DA SILVA (1923-?)	ELLA FITZGERALD (1917-1996)

Ella, Tempie, and her stepfather, Joe Da Silva, lived in Yonkers, one of the largest cities in New York. In 1923, Ella's half-sister Frances was born.

The family did not have much money. Ella did not have pretty clothes. She did not care. She was happy going to school and playing with her friends. Ella went to public school. She sang in the school's glee club. A glee club is like a choir.

Ella's neighborhood was **racially mixed**. This means that families of all different backgrounds were neighbors, including Black and white families. Most of the families were poor. All the children played together.

Ella had a lot of friends in the neighborhood. She was shy with people she did not know, but not with her friends. Ella was always goofing around with them and singing and dancing. She told them she was going to be famous one day.

Ella danced all the time. She and her friend Charles learned all the new dances. Clubs in

Yonkers paid them to dance for customers.

Sometimes Ella and her friends would take the train to Harlem to watch shows at the Apollo Theater. The Apollo is a famous music hall in New York City. Many Black singers, dancers, and comedians have performed there. During the week, the theater held **amateur** shows so people like Ella could perform.

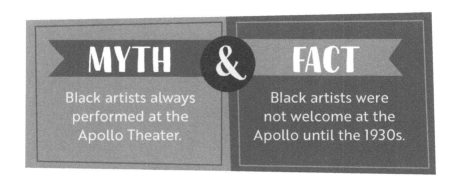

MYTH & FACT

Black artists always performed at the Apollo Theater.

Black artists were not welcome at the Apollo until the 1930s.

Staying Strong

When Ella was fifteen, her mother, Tempie, died. It was 1932. Ella stayed with her stepfather until her aunt Virginia took Ella to live with her family in Harlem. When her stepfather died, Virginia also took in Ella's little sister, Frances.

Ella was not happy living with her aunt. She missed her mother's love and care. Ella had been an excellent student, but she stopped going to school every day, and her grades went down. She

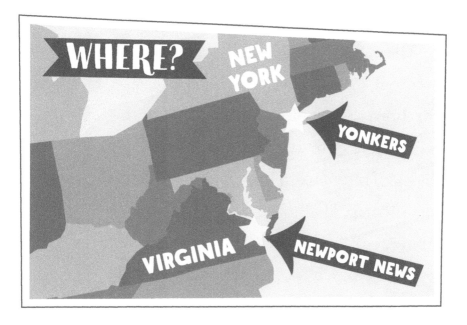

JUMP
—IN THE—
THINK
TANK

Can you think of a time when you or a friend were not treated fairly? What did you or your friend do?

even did things that were not legal to make money.

Ella got in trouble with the police. She was sent to the New York Training School for Girls. It was a **reform school** and a horrible place. Black girls were not treated well. They were separated from the white girls. Black girls were put in worse buildings. If they misbehaved, their punishment was harder.

Ella ran away. She went back to Harlem, but not to her aunt's house. She knew people would go there to look for her.

Ella had to live on her own. She did not have a home. Things were hard, but she knew she could not give up. She had to find a way to take care of herself.

There were a lot of street performers in New York City. Singers and dancers would find a spot to

perform. They would put
out a tin cup. If people
liked the performances,
they would stop and put
money in the cup.

So, Ella became a
street performer. She
made money by dancing on the street for tips.
She still loved dancing and performing, even
if it was just for change in a tin cup. Little did
she know that before long, her whole life would
change completely.

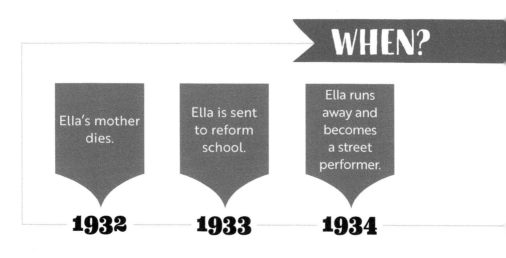

WHEN?

Ella's mother dies.	Ella is sent to reform school.	Ella runs away and becomes a street performer.
1932	**1933**	**1934**

CHAPTER 3

ELLA'S BIG

BREAK

The Apollo

Ella had been performing on the street since she ran away from reform school. Things changed when she was picked to be in the talent show at the Apollo Theater.

When you are in a talent show at the Apollo, you get to perform with famous bands. Benny Carter's band was playing music for the **contestants** the night Ella was in the show.

When it was Ella's turn to perform, she was too afraid to dance. The performers before her were also dancers. Ella knew that they were better than she was. She started singing instead.

When Benny watched Ella perform, he was surprised by how she looked. She was homeless. She was living on the street, and she was not always able to take baths. That night, she was wearing old clothes and men's shoes.

Ella's decision to sing instead of dance was the best decision she ever made. When she sang, Benny could not believe his ears. He thought she was great.

Benny introduced Ella to people in the music business. He also set up an **audition** for her with Fletcher Henderson. Fletcher was one of the greatest big-band leaders around. Benny used to work for him.

When Fletcher saw Ella, he did not like the way she looked and refused to hire her.

Ella did not let that stop her. She entered more talent shows and kept winning. In January 1935, she entered a talent show at the Harlem Opera House. Ella won there, too.

As part of her prize, Ella got to perform there for one week. In a few months, Ella had gone from performing on the street to singing in the Harlem Opera House. And she was still only a teenager!

 ## **Working the Circuit**

Around the time that Ella started winning talent shows, she met Chick Webb. In 1935, Chick was trying to make his band more popular.

He wanted to play the kind of music that made people dance. Chick started looking for a female singer to sing upbeat songs. He already had a male singer, Charles Linton. The problem was Charles sang only slow songs.

One of Chick's band members found Ella and brought her to meet Chick. Ella was still living on the street. When Chick saw her, he judged her for her dirty clothes and men's shoes. But she was so talented that he gave her a chance.

Chick brought Ella to sing with the band at Yale University in New Haven. If the students

liked her, she had a job. The students liked Ella. Chick kept his word and hired her. He paid her $12.50 per week. This was Ella's very first job, and she loved it.

JUMP
−IN THE−
THINK
TANK

What is something you would like to be the first person to do?

Ella met wonderful people in the band. Charles Linton liked Ella and was kind to her. He helped her find a place to live. For the first time in a long time, Ella had a home.

Sandy Williams, who played trombone in the band, was also kind to Ella. He treated her like she was his child. He taught her how to dress and take care of herself. No one had done that for Ella in a long time.

Ella listened to him and the other band members. She wanted to learn. She knew it was important to know how to act on stage and how to dress when performing.

> I think it's a wonderful thing
> to know that you can live in the
> streets of America and pull yourself
> up with a little help from someone
> and make it to the top.
>
> **—CHARLES LINTON**

Chick began to like her, too. He offered her a contract to join the band. When Ella signed the contract, she made history. She was the first Black woman hired to be a member of a famous big band.

WHEN?

Ella wins the talent show at the Apollo Theater.	Ella wins the talent show at the Harlem Opera House.	Ella starts singing with the Chick Webb band.
1934	**1935**	**1935**

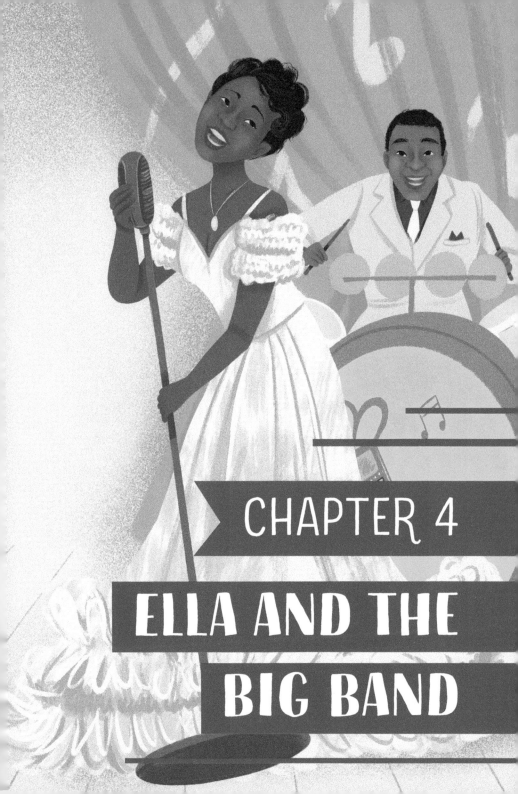

CHAPTER 4

ELLA AND THE BIG BAND

A Little Yellow Basket

When Ella sang, people danced and moved to the beat. She loved being on stage and inspiring people to dance. Ella was happy with the Chick Webb band. Chick helped her and looked after her. She was still a young singer, and he taught her how to act in the music business.

Chick was glad that he hired Ella. He knew she was the right singer to turn his band into a popular dance band. And she did!

The Chick Webb band performed all over. But they played at the Savoy Ballroom in Harlem more than anywhere else.

The Savoy Ballroom was a place people went for music and dancing. It was where you would see the latest swing dance, like the **Lindy Hop**. It was the perfect place for Ella to sing.

Unlike other places in the country, there was no segregation at the Savoy. Black people and

white people danced together. Ella sang swing, and the dancers loved it.

Ella was a very special singer. Her voice was clear. When she sang, you could understand every word.

Ella was so talented, Chick put her on recordings the band made with Decca Records. Her first **record** was "Love and Kisses" in 1935. It did not become a big hit. But it gave Ella confidence. Two years later, she recorded

Ella made bold choices, like singing when she could have danced and making a whole song out of a nursery rhyme. What is a bold decision that you made? Why was it bold?

"A-Tisket, A-Tasket." That was her first hit record.

"A-Tisket, A-Tasket" is an old nursery rhyme about a little girl who has lost her basket. It was Ella's idea to make a song out of a nursery rhyme.

That was another great decision. The song became the number-one song in the country. One million copies of the record were sold. The song made Chick and Ella famous. It made Ella a star.

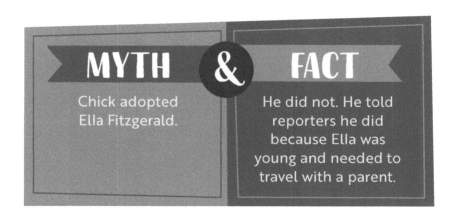

MYTH & FACT

MYTH	FACT
Chick adopted Ella Fitzgerald.	He did not. He told reporters he did because Ella was young and needed to travel with a parent.

Ella Fitzgerald and Her Famous Orchestra

Ella and Chick were great friends, but sadly, he passed away a year after they made "A-Tisket, A-Tasket."

When Chick died, the band was on their way to Montgomery, Alabama, to perform without him. Cell phones and social media had not been invented, so no one was able to tell them about Chick. When the band arrived in Montgomery, they went straight to the stage to perform.

After the show, the audience just sat there. They did not clap or do anything. They were sad because they knew Chick had died. The band did not know what was going on. Then, someone told them about Chick's death.

Ella and the band were sad to lose Chick. He was their friend and the leader of the band. And to Ella, he was like another father. They went to his

WHERE?

NEW YORK

HARLEM

BALTIMORE

ALABAMA

MONTGOMERY

funeral in Baltimore, Maryland. A few days later, they went back to work.

At twenty-one, Ella became the bandleader. This was a lot of responsibility, so others helped her with important decisions. The name was changed to Ella Fitzgerald and Her Famous Orchestra.

The band kept performing and recorded hit songs with Decca. Ella even got a small part in a movie where she sang "A-Tisket, A-Tasket."

But the band was different without Chick. The band members no longer felt like they were part of a big family. Ella tried to keep them together. But after a while, they started leaving to join

other groups. When the United States entered
World War II in 1941, some of them even had to
join the army to fight.

The band broke up in 1942. Ella became a
solo artist.

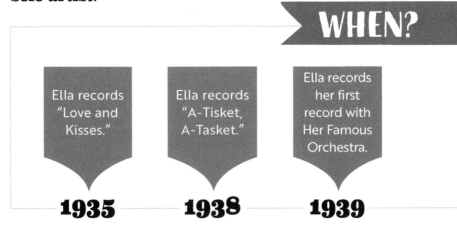

WHEN?

Ella records
"Love and
Kisses."

Ella records
"A-Tisket,
A-Tasket."

Ella records
her first
record with
Her Famous
Orchestra.

1935 — **1938** — **1939**

CHAPTER 5
SOARING TO
NEW HEIGHTS

A New Vocal Style

When Ella became a solo artist, the music world was starting to change. First, World War II made people want a different kind of music. People were missing their family members who were fighting in the war. The country was no longer in the mood for fast dance music. Big bands began to play more bebop and jazz.

Then, in August 1942, the American Federation of Musicians **union** went on **strike**. Union members refused to go to music studios for recording sessions until they received better pay. Without musicians to play for them, many singers could not make new recordings.

Ella went a whole year without making any new records. For the first time since she started singing and performing, she was not popular.

JUMP
—IN THE—
THINK
TANK

Think back to when you were a year younger. Do you still like the same kind of music? What is your favorite music or song now? Why?

But Ella did not worry. She used the time to experiment with new and more popular singing styles. She sang more bebop and scat.

Scat singing is a form of jazz where the vocalist sings syllables instead of words. It can sound like "doo be be, shoo, bop, ooh, dee, doo, sha-bam."

No one is sure who created scat singing, but Louis Armstrong made it popular. Louis sang jazz and played the trumpet. When he could not remember the words to a song called "Heebie Jeebies," he sang syllables to the beat of the music. His musicians loved it. They kept the syllables in, and the song was a hit.

The Queen of Scat

In 1945, Ella recorded "Flying Home." She had been playing around with the song for two years. The single showed that she could sing jazz and scat, but she still had more to learn.

Ella tried to learn as much as she could from the musicians she traveled with. Sometimes the musicians got together for **jam sessions**. Ella would join them and practice her scat singing.

> A lot of singers . . . refuse to look for new ideas and new outlets, so they fall by the wayside . . . I'm going to try to find out the new ideas before the others do.

Those jam sessions must have helped Ella, because she became one of the best scat singers in the country. When people listened to her, they were impressed by how well she could move her voice up and down. It wasn't like anything they'd ever heard before. It sounded like a musical instrument!

In 1946, Ella went on tour with Dizzy Gillespie. Dizzy was a very famous trumpet player and one of the first people to play bebop.

While touring with Dizzy, Ella started dating Ray Brown, a bass player. He and Ella got married in December 1947. That same month, she recorded "How High the Moon." It was one of her greatest scat songs, and it made her even more famous. Ray played bass on the recording.

In 1949, Ella joined Norman Granz's Jazz at the Philharmonic (or JATP) tour. JATP concerts were **multiracial** jazz shows with famous musicians like Louis Armstrong.

They made jazz popular around the world. When Ella joined the tour, it put her on the path to even greater things.

Ray and Ella later adopted a son. After a few years, they realized being married was not good for a couple that was always traveling. They sometimes traveled together, but a lot of the time they traveled separately. They ended the marriage in 1953. However, they remained good friends and sometimes performed together.

WHEN?

World War II ends.

Ella records "How High the Moon."

Ella becomes part of the Jazz at the Philharmonic tour.

1945 — **1947** — **1949**

CHAPTER 6
EVERYONE KNOWS ELLA

Topping the Charts

Ella liked working with Norman Granz. In December 1953, Norman became Ella's manager. Her career took off. Norman was one of the best record producers in the country. He arranged for Ella to perform in better places than the person who managed her career before him.

In 1954, he and Marilyn Monroe, a popular white actress, convinced the Mocambo club to book Ella for a show. The Mocambo was a

famous nightclub in Hollywood, California. Big stars performed there, but the club had never had a jazz singer.

When Ella performed at the

Mocambo, Marilyn made sure she was in the audience. She also made sure her celebrity friends were there, too. The audience loved Ella so much the owner had to book her for more nights.

MYTH & FACT

The Mocambo club originally did not want to book Ella because she was a Black woman.

The Mocambo club did not want to book her because she was a jazz singer.

Ella's career was soaring. That same year, *Metronome* and *DownBeat* magazines named her Best Female Singer in the country.

In July 1954, Ella made her first trip to Australia. On her way there, she had to change planes in Honolulu, Hawaii. There was some confusion, and Ella was not allowed to get on the plane in Honolulu. Ella and those traveling with her were Black. They all said the airline discriminated against them. The airline said it was just a mistake with their tickets. Norman, who always fought against segregation and discrimination, sued the airline. They came to an agreement, and the airline **compensated** Ella and the others for the way they were treated.

Ella didn't let the experience stop her from performing. When she arrived in Australia a day later, more than 1,000 people were at the airport to greet her. She performed in the cities of Sydney, Melbourne, and Brisbane. The fans there loved her, too.

Verve Records

JUMP
—IN THE—
THINK
TANK

In 1955, Norman made a deal to get Ella away from Decca Records. He wanted her to record with his company, Verve Records. Even though she sold twenty-two million records with Decca, Norman never thought she achieved as much as she could.

If you went to Australia, what is something you would like to see that you probably cannot see in the United States?

Ella decided to leave Decca and sign with Verve. In February 1956, Ella recorded *Ella Fitzgerald Sings the Cole Porter Song Book*. It was the first of her eight albums in the Great American Songbook series. A songbook is a collection of songs by great songwriters. The songs are popular year after year. They never get old. People of all ages like them.

Ella never talked about her move from Decca to Verve. She must have been pleased, because she enjoyed making her songbook albums. She was happy that she was able to record with Louis Armstrong and other great jazz musicians.

Ella was a singing sensation, but she also appeared on popular television shows. Norman even got her a part in her second film, *Pete Kelly's Blues*. She played a nightclub singer.

In 1958, Ella won the Grammy Award for Best Female Vocal Performance

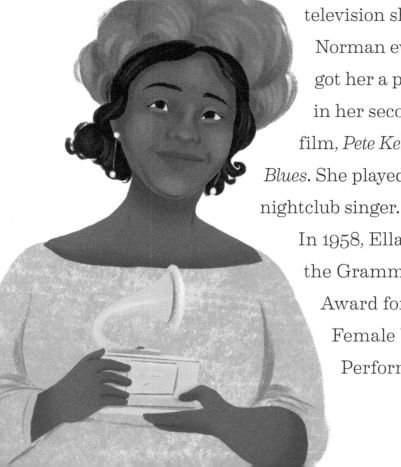

for her Irving Berlin songbook. She also won for Best Jazz Vocal Performance for her Duke Ellington songbook.

The Grammy Awards were created in 1958 to honor musicians, singers, and songwriters. Ella made history by winning a Grammy the first year the awards were given out. She also made history by being the first Black woman to win and by being the first person to win two awards in one year.

Ella won two Grammy Awards the next year as well.

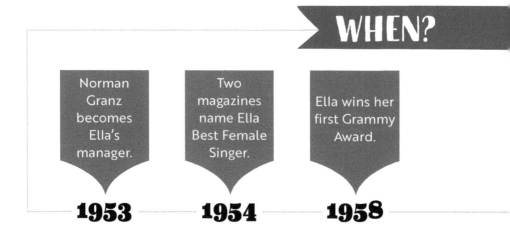

WHEN?

Norman Granz becomes Ella's manager.	Two magazines name Ella Best Female Singer.	Ella wins her first Grammy Award.
1953	**1954**	**1958**

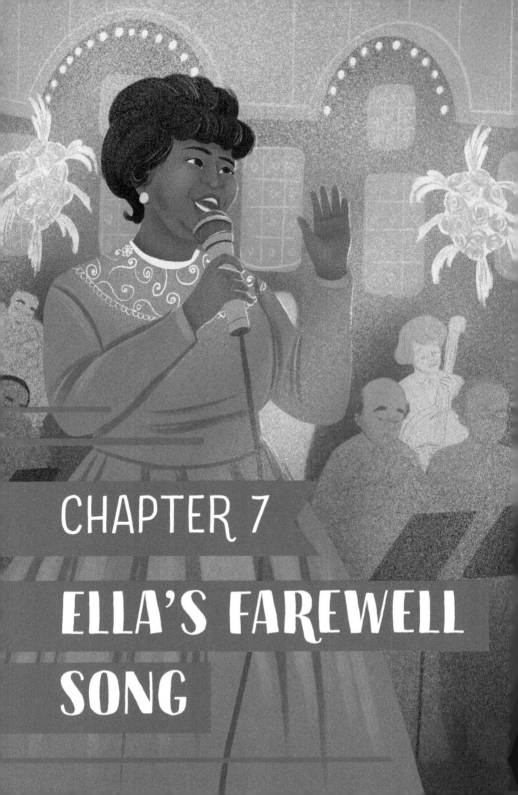

CHAPTER 7

ELLA'S FAREWELL
SONG

All That Jazz

In the 1970s, Ella began having problems with her health. She had earned a great deal of money and did not need to work. But Ella could not stop. She had been singing and performing for so long that she did not want to do anything else.

Musicians in every music style wanted to perform with her. In 1973, she was the guest soloist with several **symphony orchestras**. Unfortunately, none of those performances were recorded. However, when she sang with the Boston Pops, it was on television.

Ella kept winning Grammy Awards. During the 1976 Grammy ceremony, she sang a **duet** with Mel Tormé. Mel was also a jazz singer and always wanted to perform with Ella. The president of the Grammys said Ella and Mel got the longest **standing ovation** he had ever seen.

That same year, Ella sang at the White House for President Gerald Ford and his guests.

Ella made her final album in 1989. The record was *All That Jazz*. It won her another Grammy for Best Jazz Vocal Performance.

In 1992, Ella performed at the Music Hall Center for the Performing Arts in Detroit, Michigan. It was her final performance. She had had a long career, and Ella was proud.

As Ella grew older, she had several operations for her health. After a long and brilliant life, she passed away on June 15, 1996.

Ella's Legacy

Ella was one of the greatest singers the world has ever known. She recorded over 300 songs and sold more than forty million albums. Ella performed and entertained for more than seventy years. She is one of the few people in the world recognized by just her first name.

If you could choose an organization to help, which one would you pick? What would you do to help them?

Ella did not just entertain. She helped people as well. Ella always donated to organizations that helped children. In 1993, she used her own money to create the Ella Fitzgerald Charitable Foundation.

It isn't where you came from, it's where you're going that counts.

People all over the world respected Ella's talent. Ella won many awards during her career. She was the first woman to receive the National Endowment for the Arts Jazz Masters Fellowship, the highest honor given to a jazz artist.

Ella also won a Lifetime Achievement Award from the **Kennedy Center** in 1979. Years later, President Reagan presented her with the **National Medal of Arts**. At the very end of her career, in 1992, Ella won the highest honor a person can get in the United States: She won the Presidential Medal of Freedom.

Ella is celebrated and remembered in museums around the country. In 2007, the United States Postal Service created a stamp in her honor.

Someone once said Ella's voice was **eternal**. That must be true because she was popular year after year. Between 1958 and 1990, she received thirteen Grammy Awards. That shows that people of all ages love and value her music.

By the end of her career, Ella's fans had given her several nicknames to celebrate her talents and achievements. She was called the First Lady of Song, the Queen of Jazz, and Lady Ella. People still celebrate her as one of the best jazz musicians of all time.

WHEN?

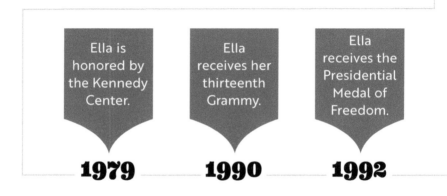

1979	1990	1992
Ella is honored by the Kennedy Center.	Ella receives her thirteenth Grammy.	Ella receives the Presidential Medal of Freedom.

CHAPTER 8

SO...WHO WAS ELLA FITZGERALD?

Challenge Accepted!

Now that you have learned about Ella Fitzgerald's life, let's test your new knowledge with a little "who, what, when, where, why, and how" quiz. Feel free to look back in the text to find the answers if you need to, but try to remember first!

1 **Where was Ella born?**
→ A   Petersburg, Virginia
→ B   Wilmington, Delaware
→ C   Tuskegee, Alabama
→ D   Newport News, Virginia

What war was the United States fighting in when Ella was born?
→ A   Korean War
→ B   Vietnam War
→ C   World War I
→ D   World War II

3 **What city did Ella and her mother move to?**

→ A   Richmond

→ B   Yonkers

→ C   New Haven

→ D   Baltimore

Where did Ella win her first talent show?

→ A   Harlem Opera House

→ B   Apollo Theater

→ C   Savoy Ballroom

→ C   Lincoln Center

5 **Who was the first person to give Ella a job?**

→ A   Chick Webb

→ B   Benny Carter

→ C   Dizzy Gillespie

→ D   Charles Linton

6 **What was Ella's first hit record?**

→ A "Love and Kisses"

→ B "The Best is Yet to Come"

→ C "A-Tisket, A-Tasket"

→ D "Cheek to Cheek"

How old was Ella when she entered her first talent show?

→ A 17

→ B 21

→ C 15

→ D 16

8 **Which president presented Ella the National Medal of Arts?**

→ A President Clinton

→ B President Carter

→ C President Ford

→ D President Reagan

How many Grammy Awards did Ella win?

→ A   Five

→ B   Thirteen

→ C   Two

→ D   Eight

10   What company did Ella record with after Decca?

→ A   Columbia

→ B   Atlantic

→ C   Verve

→ D   Pablo

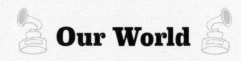 Our World

How has Ella's work changed our world today?
Let's take a look at her lasting impact.

→ The Ella Fitzgerald Charitable Foundation continues to
support children in need. Every year, it provides health
care, food, shelter, and counseling to people who need it.
It also wants to teach kids to love music and reading.

→ Have you ever heard of Andra Day, Ledisi, and Lady
Gaga? All three of these popular singers say that
Ella Fitzgerald inspired them. Young singers around
the world are continually influenced and inspired by
her music.

→ In 2003, the Library of Congress added *Ella Fitzgerald
Sings the Cole Porter Song Book* to its list of historically
important recordings. Ella officially made history!

→ Ella's songs are still being released today. On what
would have been her one hundredth birthday, Verve
released an album of her most famous songs. They called
it *100 Songs for a Centennial*.

JUMP
—IN THE—
THINK TANK
FOR

MORE!

Now let's think a little more about Ella's life and influence. How will she inspire you?

→ Ella was always willing to change if it was better for her. At her first talent show, she decided to sing instead of dance. When people stopped listening to her songs, she changed what she sang. Why is it important to change and try different things?

→ Ella did not stop performing, even though she did not need to work. What is something you would keep doing no matter what?

→ Ella performed as a soloist and as a member of a band. Do you prefer working by yourself or with others?

→ When Ella got famous, she decided that she wanted to give back to people in need. If you had a lot of money to give, who would you want to help?

Glossary

amateur: A person who is a beginner, still learning, and not getting paid

audition: Try out for something

compensate: Pay someone to make up for something that was done to them

contestant: A person in a contest

declare war: Make the decision to go to war against a country

duet: When two artists sing together

eternal: Having no end

jam sessions: Times when musicians get together to practice and try new music and songs

jazz: Music that started in New Orleans with Black singers and musicians putting different types of music together and making up new sounds as they went along

Jim Crow laws: Laws that made it legal to separate people by race and the color of their skin

Kennedy Center: A place that supports and honors the best performers in the world

Lindy Hop: A type of dance where dancers hold hands and move around fast, kicking their legs out and throwing their arms around

multiracial: Made up of several races of people

National Medal of Arts: The highest award given by the United States for excellent work in the arts and music

racially mixed: When different races of people are together in one place or area

racial segregation: Separating people by race or the color of their skin

record: What music was put on before compact discs

reform school: A place where teenagers are sent when they break the law

solo artist: A singer who works alone

standing ovation: Standing up and clapping for a long time

streetcar: A kind of bus that runs on rails on the street

strike: Refusing to work until certain conditions change

symphony orchestra: A large group of about one hundred musicians playing together

union: Workers who join together to protect the rights of all of them

Bibliography

Billboard. Accessed June 16, 2021. Billboard.com/music/ella-fitzgerald /chart-history/traditional-jazz-albums/song/324912.

Brian Linehan's *City Lights*. "Ella Fitzgerald Interview 1974." Accessed May 19, 2021. YouTube.com/watch?v=dunLgfk3XWI.

Clark, Dr. Ian D. *Ella Fitzgerald in Australia: A History*. Scotts Valley, CA: CreateSpace, 2014. Kindle.

Ella Fitzgerald. Accessed May 22, 2021. EllaFitzgerald.com.

Grammy Awards. "Ella Fitzgerald." Accessed May 22, 2021. Grammy.com /grammys/artists/ella-fitzgerald/16685.

Immarigeon, Russ. "The 'Ungovernable' Ella Fitzgerald." *Prison Public Memory Project* (blog). October 29, 2014. PrisonPublicMemory.org/blog/2014 /the-ungovernable-ella-fitzgerald.

Mark, Geoffrey. *ELLA: A Biography of the Legendary Ella Fitzgerald*. Centennial Birthday Edition. New York: Ultimate Symbol, 2018.

National Endowment for the Arts. "Ella Fitzgerald." Accessed June 16, 2021. Arts.gov/honors/jazz/ella-fitzgerald.

Nicholson, Stuart. *Ella Fitzgerald: The Complete Biography*. New York: Routledge, 2004.

The Great American Songbook Foundation. "Ella Sings the Songbook." Accessed June 26, 2021. TheSongbook.org/ellafitzgerald.

Virginia Museum of History and Culture. "Jim Crow to Civil Rights in Virginia." Accessed May 23, 2021. VirginiaHistory.org/learn /jim-crow-civil-rights-virginia.

About the Author

Kathy Trusty is an independent historian, Black history educator, and nonfiction children's book author. She is the founder of Black History Ed Zone LLC, a Black history education company that produces Black history products for students in grades K–8. Kathy is also a speaker with Delaware Humanities on African Americans and the Civil War. She is the author of *Black Inventors: 15 Inventions That Changed the World*, published by Rockridge Press in 2021. She is also the author of *I AM BLACK I AM PROUD I AM THEM: Black History ABCs*, which was published by Black History Ed Zone in 2020.

About the Illustrator

Sawyer Cloud is a self-taught artist living in Madagascar, her native country. Passionate about the visual arts, she learned illustration through personal research and work experience. When not drawing, she is singing and wearing her favorite fairy costume. She lives with her family and her two pets, Arya the dog and Potter the cat. Find her at www.Sawyer.Cloud.

WHO WILL INSPIRE YOU NEXT?

EXPLORE A WORLD OF HEROES AND ROLE MODELS IN
***THE STORY OF*...** BIOGRAPHY SERIES FOR NEW READERS.

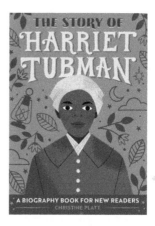

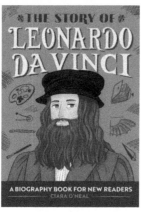

LOOK FOR THIS SERIES
WHEREVER BOOKS AND EBOOKS ARE SOLD

Alexander Hamilton	Jane Goodall
Albert Einstein	Barack Obama
Martin Luther King Jr.	Helen Keller
George Washington	Marie Curie